Louise McKay

SUMMERSDALE

Summersdale Publishers Ltd
46 West Street
Chichester
PO19 1RP
UK

www.summersdale.com

ISBN 1 84024 271 X

Printed and bound in Great Britain

Cartoons by Kate Taylor

YOU KNOW YOUR BOYFRIEND'S USELESS WHEN . . .

He claims to have a keen interest in meteorology…especially golden showers.

He tries to convince you that you need your tongue pierced…claiming it will heighten sexual pleasure for you too. You can't quite compute that one.

He is forever hiding your baby sister's powdered milk…in order to force your mother to breastfeed in public.

He brags about being able to muff dive off a 20-foot board. He's missing the point…quite literally.

He glues the toilet seat up, forcing you to sit on his ammonia-ridden dribble.

He uses the kitchen sink as a urinal, which would be okay if he weren't doing the washing up simultaneously.

He insists on upgrading to a broadband
Internet connection. Need I say more?

He likes to think of himself as a sex god, even though most of your friends mistake him for a sumo wrestler.

YOU KNOW YOUR BOYFRIEND'S USELESS WHEN . . .

He feeds you pies and cakes in an attempt to get you too fat for anyone else.

He regularly visits strip clubs with his mates, but won't even let you watch *The Full Monty*.

YOU KNOW YOUR BOYFRIEND'S USELESS WHEN . . .

He thinks you should be grateful that he can do 'it' in just under a minute. With practise, he says, you'll get better too.

YOU KNOW YOUR BOYFRIEND'S USELESS WHEN . . .

He refuses to fund your career ambitions as a full-time shopper.

The closest he's ever come to whispering sweet nothings in your ear is snoring, grunting and groaning in his sleep.

He is squeamish about the C-word: commitment has always nauseated him.

YOU KNOW YOUR BOYFRIEND'S USELESS WHEN . . .

The longest word he knows is cellulite.

He has been known to confuse you with his blow-up doll…you wondered why he sometimes tries to deflate you before running you under the hot tap.

He thinks flowers are just for funerals. It's all the more worrying when he buys you a wreath on Valentine's Day.

He's not once noticed your hairstyle… not even when you swapped your waist-length locks for the *GI Jane* shaved look. However, he's always first to notice if you've had a Brazilian Wax.

23

YOU KNOW YOUR BOYFRIEND'S USELESS WHEN . . .

He buys you weight loss manuals for Christmas.

He talks publicly about the size of your *twat* and expects you to be flattered.

YOU KNOW YOUR BOYFRIEND'S USELESS WHEN . . .

He complains of RSI of the tongue.

The alphabet seems only to consist of three letters…S E X.

YOU KNOW YOUR BOYFRIEND'S USELESS WHEN . . .

During lovemaking he cries out *Jordan* by mistake…and naturally you don't believe his claims that he's always wanted to visit the Middle Eastern state.

He pays for you to have a boob job…even though your knockers are already a hefty 32FF.

YOU KNOW YOUR BOYFRIEND'S USELESS WHEN . . .

He thinks *clitoris* is Latin for myth.

He suggests you have a
hysterectomy…so that he can have his
wicked way with you 365 days a year
without the hassle of contraception.

YOU KNOW YOUR BOYFRIEND'S USELESS WHEN . . .

Even after being partners for five years, he still needs an A-Z to find your G-spot. And a compass and crampons.

YOU KNOW YOUR BOYFRIEND'S USELESS WHEN . . .

He calls himself a researcher...never mind that he's researching *hot asian chicks* on the Internet.

He puts your names forward as candidates for *Temptation Island..*

Men are usually tit men or bum men.
Your boyfriend is just a twat, man.

He recognises period pain. For him it is a total pain in the arse…he has to visit a prozzie for that week.

He has had so many girlfriends that he refers to you by number, not name. He even considers installing a barcode system.

YOU KNOW YOUR BOYFRIEND'S USELESS WHEN . . .

He is incapable of looking your female friends in the eye and would only recognise them by the shape of their breasts.

YOU KNOW YOUR BOYFRIEND'S USELESS WHEN . . .

All the underwear he buys you is transparent…just like him.

The only jewellery he has ever given you was a pearl necklace…and a tissue to wipe it off with.

YOU KNOW YOUR BOYFRIEND'S USELESS WHEN . . .

He forgets your name in front of your family, but is happy to recall your most recent sexual act over the Sunday Roast.

His idea of romance is to offer you the choice between a paper bag or doggy-style sex.

All the names in his address book turn out to be premium rate sex lines.

The *Gimp* scene in *Pulp Fiction* turns him on just a bit too much.

YOU KNOW YOUR BOYFRIEND'S USELESS WHEN . . .

He tries to persuade you that three inches is more than most women dream of.

He forgets your birthday, the colour of your eyes and your middle name…but is always the first to recall your cup size.

His idea of unconditional love is that you accept his farting, belching and masturbating...plus the things he does in private.

During Sunday lunch at your family's house, he suggests a wet t-shirt competition and proceeds to pour gravy down your mum's top.

He sulks for days when you tell him that you have no intention of starving yourself to supermodel waifdom just for him.

YOU KNOW YOUR BOYFRIEND'S USELESS WHEN . . .

You ask him to flick your bean and he turns up with a can of *Heinz*.

YOU KNOW YOUR BOYFRIEND'S USELESS WHEN . . .

He doesn't believe in after-shave...
surely his bodily smells are enough to
drive anyone crazy?

YOU KNOW YOUR BOYFRIEND'S USELESS WHEN . . .

He refers without irony to the garden shed as his masturbatory retreat.

He insists you maintain a perfect size
10 figure and yet expects you to orgasm
at the sight of his portly beer gut.

YOU KNOW YOUR BOYFRIEND'S USELESS WHEN . . .

He encourages you to take up more sports… topless darts, bottomless archery, full-frontal falconry and other well known past times.

YOU KNOW YOUR BOYFRIEND'S USELESS WHEN . . .

He takes you to a nudist camp…but spends all his time inside the tent peering through the flaps, so to speak.

YOU KNOW YOUR BOYFRIEND'S USELESS WHEN . . .

You return home to find a fireman's pole installed in your bedroom…and are disappointed not to be able to find the fireman too, given your boyfriend is such an arsehole.

YOU KNOW YOUR BOYFRIEND'S USELESS WHEN . . .

He is forever trying to get inside your knickers, but you tell him there's already one arsehole in there.

You ask for something black, leather and kinky for your birthday: he buys you some blinkers from the local saddlery to stop you looking at other men.

YOU KNOW YOUR BOYFRIEND'S USELESS WHEN . . .

He buys a giant bed in the hope that you will invite all your girlfriends round for a sleepover.

He is genuinely shocked to learn that girls wee AND poo.

YOU KNOW YOUR BOYFRIEND'S USELESS WHEN . . .

He buys you a dildo and is then offended that it gives you more pleasure than his 'wham, bam, thank you ma'am' technique.

He takes you out to dinner but seems to have more to say to the attractive waitress than he does to you.

He offers to share the household chores by volunteering responsibility for the washing-up…and then buys hundreds of disposable paper plates.

YOU KNOW YOUR BOYFRIEND'S USELESS WHEN . . .

He thinks flushing the toilet is the same as cleaning it.

He thinks it is old fashioned for the man to pay for everything. Trust you to get a New Man who expects to go halves.

He's late for a date with you because *Baywatch* is on.

YOU KNOW YOUR BOYFRIEND'S USELESS WHEN . . .

The muscles in his right arm are noticeably more developed than those in his left.

YOU KNOW YOUR BOYFRIEND'S USELESS WHEN . . .

He can't see the difference between feminists and lesbians…and is always encouraging you to be the former.

He is always trying to get you and your girlfriends drunk together in the vain hope that you'll indulge in a spot of girlie fun. You and your mates continue to humour him.

He tattoos your name on his arm… which now resembles a double-page spread from the *Thompson's Directory*.

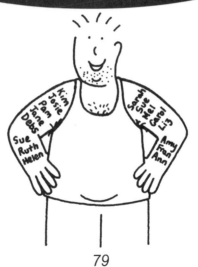

He thinks you undervalue his achievements: after all, not everyone can drink a pint and then vomit it all back into the glass. And drink it again.

YOU KNOW YOUR BOYFRIEND'S USELESS WHEN . . .

He thinks that opening an account for you at *Ann Summers* will cure your negative body image.

**YOU KNOW YOUR
BOYFRIEND'S USELESS
WHEN . . .**

He still finds the word *tampon* really funny.

YOU KNOW YOUR BOYFRIEND'S USELESS WHEN . . .

He offers to take you to see his football team play...but only on the proviso that you streak at half time.

His main source of income is by
charging his filthy-minded mates to spy
on you while you bathe. Or better still
change a tampon.

He takes up life drawing just to get you
to pose naked for him.

85

YOU KNOW YOUR BOYFRIEND'S USELESS WHEN . . .

His idea of pure, romantic extravagance is to hire ALL the dirty movies from the shop, not just one.

YOU KNOW YOUR BOYFRIEND'S USELESS WHEN . . .

He buys you subscriptions to *Maxim* and *Playboy*…and you find pictures of yourself in the *Readers Wives* section.

YOU KNOW YOUR BOYFRIEND'S USELESS WHEN . . .

He tries and fails to convince you that no condom will fit you...and you agree because they're all too big.

He can't see the point in buying you an expensive ring when he has a toolbox full of washers.

The only time he says *I love you* is when he's pissed…and that's to the male paramedic who's trying to revive him after a night in the pub.

He thinks foreplay involves two of your girlfriends joining in.

You cover yourself in chocolate sauce
in the hope that he might have a
nibble… but he puts a couple of slices
of *Mother's Pride* in the toaster instead.

He innocently claims not to notice the difference between vaginal and anal sex.

He thinks that your erogenous zone is somewhere he can't afford to travel on the *London Underground*.

YOU KNOW YOUR BOYFRIEND'S USELESS WHEN . . .

He still insists on taking advice from the other woman in his life...his mother.

He gets his best friend to end your relationship and then starts dating your best mate. Mmm, that's nice.

On your wedding day he fails to notice what you're wearing…except that it's a dress. And he only recognises that because it has easier access than your jeans.

Every headache he has is potentially meningitis, but you are told to shut the *uck up when you are bleeding to death in the road. Sweet.

YOU KNOW YOUR BOYFRIEND'S USELESS WHEN . . .

His definition of safe sex is locking the door first.

YOU KNOW YOUR BOYFRIEND'S USELESS WHEN . . .

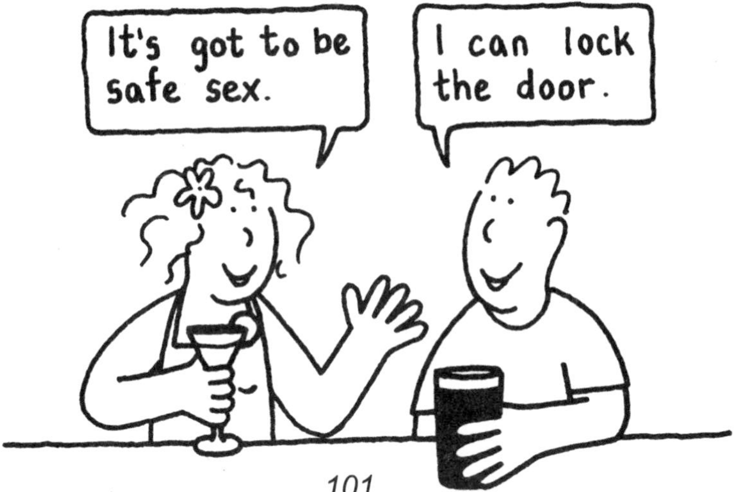

You mention your sexual peak and he thinks you're hinting at a mountaineering holiday.

He uses his nob as a millimetre stick,
not a yardstick.

He thinks *Labia Majora* and *Minora* are two small Balearic islands. They may as well be, let's face it.

YOU KNOW YOUR BOYFRIEND'S USELESS WHEN . . .

He'd be better at pinning a tail on a donkey than finding your G-spot. Come to think of it, you'd rather he spent the night with the donkey.

His ideal diet would be edible knickers.

YOU KNOW YOUR BOYFRIEND'S USELESS WHEN . . .

He thinks he is 007.

YOU KNOW YOUR BOYFRIEND'S USELESS WHEN . . .

He claims that anything pertaining to homosexual activity is abhorrent...but is more than happy to tamper with your back passage.

YOU KNOW YOUR BOYFRIEND'S USELESS WHEN . . .

He thinks the smell of pure raw sex is a turn on. Sure, but the smell of stale sweat, piss, beer and curry isn't.

His idea of doing the housework is
picking his feet up for a change.

He insists his innate map reading skills
are second to none and would rather be
stranded on the Moors than ask a girl
for directions.

YOU KNOW YOUR BOYFRIEND'S USELESS WHEN . . .

His fridge is always totally bare except for beer bottles...empty ones.

He claims he can't cook but, the minute summer arrives, spends every weekend cooking barbecued lard for his mates.

He fully advocates one-night stands
within your relationship…as long as
they're his.

He'd rather spend a night out with
Jeremy Clarkson than Claudia Schiffer.

YOU KNOW YOUR BOYFRIEND'S USELESS WHEN . . .

He is always trying to feign some fatal illness or other…just to get another glimpse of those chicks in nurses uniforms.

You tell him *brain* is spelt P-E-N-I-S. It takes him a moment or two to work that one out.

The only kitchen utensil he is familiar with is a bottle opener. Oh, and a tin opener…but only because he thinks it's some kind of kinky gynaecological instrument.

YOU KNOW YOUR BOYFRIEND'S USELESS WHEN . . .

He doesn't think about sex every 7 seconds. With him it's on the brain 24/7.

He is a control freak. A remote control freak, that is, as he won't let you watch anything other than *Men and Motors*.

EMMA BURGESS

YOU KNOW YOU'RE A
CAT LOVER
WHEN...

CAT CARE

summersdale *humour*

LOUISE McKAY

YOU KNOW YOU'RE AN
E-MAIL ADDICT
WHEN...

@

summersdale *humour*

ED COBHAM

YOU KNOW YOU'RE A
DIY ADDICT
WHEN...

summersdale *humour*

MICHELLE LEGGATT

YOU KNOW YOU'RE A
FASHION JUNKIE
WHEN...

NEW TROUSERS -
IN FASHION
ONE WEEK ONLY!

summersdale *humour*

YOU KNOW YOU'RE A COMPUTER NERD WHEN... — SUMMERSDALE

REVENGE — 101 THINGS TO DO WHEN YOU'VE BEEN DUMPED — NICK FERRIS — summersdale humour

YOU KNOW YOU'RE A MAN EATER WHEN... — EMMA BURGESS — summersdale humour

YOU KNOW YOUR DIET ISN'T WORKING WHEN... — EMMA BURGESS — summersdale humour

For the latest humour books
from Summersdale, check out